ESTHER SCHMIDT

Date: 9/

D1463278

Dwarf Rabbits

**PALM BEACH COUNTY
LIBRARY SYSTEM**

3650 Summit Boulevard
West Palm Beach, FL 33406-4198

BARRON'S

Contents

Exciting games with food keep dwarf rabbits fit and healthy.

What Dwarf Rabbits Are Like

An Indoor Paradise for Dwarf Rabbits

Outdoors—Lots of Freedom

Games, Sports, and All Kinds of Fun

THE FINELY TUNED RABBIT NOSE RELIABLY SNIFFS OUT EVERY SCENT.

What Dwarf Rabbits Are Like

They look comical, have a charming nature, and bubble with *joie de vivre*. Dwarf rabbits are totally lovable. However, these tiny friends demand specific living conditions and care that are the equal of their big cousins. Looking at their relatives living in the wild teaches a lot about dwarf rabbits' lifestyle, behavior, and needs and will provide you with lots of important information about the right way to deal with your new family members.

Senses

Rabbits are practically defenseless against their numerous predators, so they seek safety by fleeing. Their outstanding senses give them early warnings of threats to ensure their survival.

GROPING IN THE DARK

Rabbits, which are active in twilight, orient themselves in the dark using the whiskers on their upper lip, chin, and eyebrows. The whiskers are about as long as the rabbit is wide, and they function like spacers. The whiskers react to the slightest touch, indicate obstacles in a timely fashion, and indicate whether the animal can fit through a tight opening.

THE LANGUAGE OF SCENT

The 100 million olfactory cells in a rabbit's nose can perceive the faintest traces of scent. Communication takes place primarily through scents, and territory is marked with scents.

HEARING THE GRASS GROW

Rabbit ears are really high-tech auditory systems that detect even the faintest noises. The funnel-shaped ears can be aimed independently of one another and cover a 360-degree listening area. Rabbit breeds with lop ears do not hear nearly as well.

EVERYTHING IN VIEW

Rabbit eyes are located on the sides of the head and provide a perfect panoramic view. This orientation allows rabbits to detect predators at a great distance. However, the rabbits' three-dimensional vision is greatly restricted up close.

WITH A FINE TONGUE

With 8,000 taste buds on their tongue, dwarf rabbits immediately perceive whether their food is sweet, sour, bitter, or salty. However, it is significantly harder for domesticated dwarfs to distinguish between poisonous and edible plants than it is for their relatives living in the wild.

Behaviors

Dwarf rabbits display some typical and distinct behaviors that owners must take into account when these rabbits are kept as pets. This is the only way to ensure that your wards will lead a long and healthy life.

LOAFERS

Even though rabbits are very active, they enjoy their breaks. If they feel at ease, you can watch them during the day while they are relaxing and sunbathing.

CONSTANT NIBBLERS

Rabbits are hindgut fermentors that require a sufficient amount of food in order for their digestive tract to derive the nutrients that their bodies need to stay healthy. In fact, they eat up to 80 meals a day in order to keep from developing painful and life-threatening digestive conditions. Fasting can be fatal.

SPRINTERS

Rabbits are first-class sprinters and can reach speeds of 24 miles an hour (40 km/h). Nimble feet and quick reactions assure their survival. Even dwarf rabbits kept inside a house need lots of exercise.

RODENTS AND GNAWERS

A rabbit's teeth grow throughout its lifetime, up to ½ inch (15 mm) or more per month. To avoid problems, teeth must be kept short through continuous gnawing on hard food. By providing appropriate gnawing material, such as branches from fruit trees, beech trees, oaks, and hazelnut trees, you can steer their compulsion in the right direction.

TUNNELERS AND EARTH MOVERS

Digging and tunneling is a basic instinct in rabbits. It continues unabated when they are kept as pets. So always provide your dwarfs with appropriate digging opportunities.

7

Vocalizations

Rabbits cannot make any loud sounds because their enemies lurk everywhere. Nevertheless, communication among them works perfectly. Owners must listen very carefully to hear the faint sounds dwarf rabbits make.

GRINDING THE TEETH

Scarcely audible gritting and grinding of the teeth are typical sounds from a rabbit that feels comfortable, happy, and relaxed. On the other hand, a pronounced, loud grinding of the teeth signals serious pain. Accompanying symptoms frequently include apathetic behavior, a tense body, and a dull expression in the eyes. In the presence of such symptoms of illness, immediately consult a veterinarian. A quick diagnosis and treatment will reduce discomfort and increase the chances of a cure.

HUMMING WITH LOVE

A courting male rabbit expresses his readiness to mate by humming in a deep voice. After mating, he usually emits a loud grumbling sound.

DRUMMING IN THE FACE OF DANGER

The rabbit drums on the ground with its hind feet and alerts its comrades when danger is at hand. Many times, this early warning system proves to be a lifesaver.

PEEPING IN DISTRESS

A gentle peeping keeps coming from the nest; the babies tirelessly call for their mother. The peeping indicates hunger, cold, and anxiety. Older animals emit this forlorn sound when they feel insecure or lonely. This occurs more when an animal is kept alone because the rabbit misses the company of other rabbits.

HISSING AS A FINAL WARNING

Soft hissing indicates discontent. Stubborn rabbits are put into their place with a sharp hissing or growling. If the threat doesn't work, an attack may follow. The owner also needs to be alert to this.

Body Language

The distinct body language of dwarf rabbits not only lets them communicate with other dwarf rabbits but also indicates an individual's health and emotions. The rabbits' body language indicates comfort and pure joy but also advertises when they are feeling stress, anxiety, and pain.

MARKING OWNERSHIP

By rubbing its chin, the rabbit emits a scent that confirms its ownership claim. Spraying urine is another typical behavior used to mark territory.

PERFECT GROOMING

Rabbits are exceptionally clean animals, and they spend lots of time in intensive grooming. They need help with grooming only in exceptional cases, for example when their agility declines in old age or when they are ill. In the evening, it is often possible to see rabbits groom one another. This activity fosters a sense of community and strengthens family ties.

MOUNTING FOR DOMINANCE

Mounting is not just for reproduction; it is also used in establishing the pecking order. It is even possible to see females and young rabbits do this when they are trying to earn a place in the upper echelons.

SHRINKING IN FEAR

Crouching and shrinking are an expression of great fear. If the closest hiding spot is too far away or if all retreat paths are blocked, the rabbit presses itself flat to the ground, lays its ears back, remains totally motionless, and hopes that it is invisible to its enemy.

ROLLING BLISSFULLY

Rabbits like to dig hollows in the ground. They roll in them and toss from one side to the other on their back. Rolling expresses the most profound sense of well-being. Since rabbits are defenseless when on their back, they roll only when they feel totally secure.

9

PAW CHECK—EXCESSIVELY LONG CLAWS
MUST BE TRIMMED REGULARLY.

An Indoor Paradise for Dwarf Rabbits

The days of boring pens are long gone! Thanks to multifunctional modules, you can offer your dwarfs a life filled with variety that meets their needs even indoors and in limited space.

The exuberant dwarfs also enjoy their rest breaks.

Lots of buddies, room to romp, hideouts, and places to cuddle—these are what make rabbits happy.

A Comfortable Life in the Land of Dwarfs

In order for your dwarf rabbits to feel comfortable living with you, you need to learn about their lifestyle and meet their needs (see front inside flap). Unfortunately, two basic needs are not always appreciated and are often neglected by inexperienced rabbit owners. First, rabbits need to be part of a group in order to be happy. Second, along with group living, rabbits need lots of exercise.

At Least a Pair

Rabbits are gregarious, outgoing animals with distinctive social behavior. Exuberant racing around, mutual grooming, and an occasional chat in rabbit talk are simply part of rabbit life. Spare the animals from solitary confinement. Happy dwarf rabbits must live in pairs and, if there is enough room, in a group. That's the only way they can develop their zest for life and astound us with their varied repertory of behaviors.

ALWAYS ON THE GO

Wild rabbits lead a life full of exciting and sometimes dangerous adventure. Every day brings new challenges. Any rabbit that does not overcome them doesn't have much hope of survival. So from the time they are little, rabbits rehearse for the emergency. Their most important training exercise is the sprint combined with quick changes in direction and dazzling jumping performances. Even though our dwarfs don't have to flee predators at home, their inborn need for exercise remains intact. It is important for the animals to play it out fully. So you must provide an open area of at least 36 square feet (2 sq m) per rabbit and hours of additional physical exercise. This is the only way to keep the animals fit so they can enjoy the best of health into advanced age.

A BETTER LIFE

There are three appropriate indoor living conditions, which depend on the amount of space available. Dwarfs can run free inside the house, in a rabbit room, or in a pen inside a room.

Running free indoors: Running free inside the house offers the dwarfs all kinds of variety and freedom to move around. However, it requires extensive security measures and vigilance, plus understanding from the whole family and from visitors.

A rabbit room: The dwarfs have their own area: a room exclusively for the rabbits! This is, of course, the optimal situation. The dwarfs feel on top of the world since everything can be tailored to their needs. Dangers are manageable and can be neutralized effectively.

A pen: The most common living arrangement for rabbits is a pen inside a room. The space requirement is reasonable, and a pen can be installed even in small homes. The dwarfs can romp around inside the defined area and take an active part in their family life. A pen with movable sections allows you to change the sphere of action for the troop at will.

Everything Secure?

- Run electric cords through conduits.
- Remove poisonous plants.
- Keep cleaning agents, medications, knives, and scissors locked up.
- Secure fire and cooking areas.
- Remove fabrics in which the animals' claws could get caught.
- Keep the windows closed when the rabbits are running around free.
- Keep cats, dogs, and other pets out of the rabbit room.

The sand shell is a real rabbit paradise. The opening of the shell is adjustable.

Types of Pens

You can find commercially produced partitions for pens at pet shops. Building supply stores offer appropriate parts for making them yourself. That way, you can choose any materials, shapes, and colors you want. Look for sufficient height, good workmanship, and ease of handling.

Metallic look: Pet shops sell wire mesh (photo 4) for outdoor pens. This mesh works well indoors too. It is light and easy to handle. It is durable and comes in various heights. Expandable push-fit systems, which are easy to put together and take apart, are another good choice. For large pens, an attachment point to the floor should be added to the wall attachment to provide for greater stability.

The right track: Decorative wooden fences (photo 2), which are available at building supply stores, are good choices for delimiting pens. You can buy ready-made sections of fence or assemble the boards yourself. With homemade fences, you can determine the space between the boards and thus make sure that no dwarf can squeeze through or get its head stuck. If necessary, you can secure the lower part with gnaw-proof wire.

Hardwired: You can build a partition. First build several rectangular wood frames out of laths. Secure wire to them. Then simply connect the frames. If you don't want to build a partition yourself, you can use an outdoor pen from a pet shop (photo 5). Elements that are too low can simply be stood on end. Hinges are a good way to join wooden frames together. They should be installed so that the partition can be folded up like a fan. This makes the partition easier to handle and to store.

Stylish with glass: Homemade pens that incorporate glass (photo 1) provide good visibility into and out of the pen. If you use tongue and groove lumber or aluminum strips for the frame, you can easily install the panes of glass between them. Glass walls make everything seem more airy and refined. You can choose clear or lightly patterned glass. An economical variation is to use an old Plexiglas shower door instead of new glass.

Tip: Do not saw thin Plexiglas. Simply score it deeply and break it over a beam.

Nothing to sneeze at: Sturdy pieces of cardboard held together with heavy adhesive tape (photo 3) are a good makeshift arrangement that can also be used when the rabbits are out and about under supervision. When you are putting on the tape, leave a little space between the cardboard pieces. Then you can save space by simply folding the cardboard at the joints to store the partition.

Tip

Generally a height of 28–32 inches (70–80 cm) is adequate for any partitions. However, some dwarfs can jump really high and need extra-high partitions. Test the run under supervision to locate any weak spots. With a high-walled pen, don't overlook your need for easy access.

1 A see-through pen. An old shower door made of frosted glass is put to good use. The built-in door facilitates access without allowing a dwarf to sneak away. Everything folds, so it is easy to handle.

2 This decorative wood fence was put together by the owner. The necessary materials are available in any building supply store. You can tailor the height of the boards to the jumping skills of your dwarfs.

3 Even solid pieces of cardboard are usable for supervised exercise. With dwarf rabbits, things can sometimes get really rowdy.

4 Wire mesh is the standard available from pet shops. The light weight makes it easy to put together and take apart.

5 Wood frames covered with wire provide security. Here the elements of a prefabricated pen are stood on end and held together with hinges.

15

Plenty of room is available for jumping and romping.

Solid, attractive, and practical: modular elements adapt marvelously well to all space requirements.

Modules—
Very Versatile Performers

A whole array of rabbit houses are available on the market. Not all of them earn high marks for materials, everyday serviceability, and durability. With private dealers, you may hit pay dirt. However, the price is often a deal breaker. Chic modular houses that expand and fulfill every possible desire are not usually affordable. Commercial modules often form a multicolored rabbit home outfitted with practical and attractive elements but that look

cluttered. The dwarfs don't care much, of course, but many rabbit owners no longer feel at home inside their own four walls.

Homemade Modules

Homemade modules can help. They are easy to make and don't require you to be a professional carpenter. In any case making these is worth a try because the modules offer many advantages. Modules …

… allow for optimal usage of available space because module types can vary in size and shape.

… can be put together in a variety of ways: as a dwelling unit, as an observation platform, as tunnels, or as a hiding place.

… offer their inhabitants lots of variety with countless configurations.

… adapt easily in shape, color, and appearance to your home.

… are reasonably priced, easy to make, and durable.

… are usable as shelf space and even as seating for the owner because of their great sturdiness.

… are easy to keep clean. Simply separate the units from each other to clean them thoroughly. Because they are screwed together, boards that have become soiled can be easily replaced.

… can be set up as individual elements or in any arrangement you wish, including on top of one another.

… are easy to handle. They can easily be moved to another room or to a different house.

… allow for expansion of the dwarfs' living space at will.

… can be used outdoors with minimal adaptation (lower right photo, p. 49).

The Right Material

For health reasons, using untreated, solid wood is the best choice. However, it is very expensive. It also expands and shrinks so that the structures warp quickly and nothing fits anymore. The warping takes the pleasure

Tip
Some building supply stores offer a cutting service. For a small additional cost, you can even have the openings in the plywood cut. You could even borrow or rent high-quality tools to cut the openings yourself.

out of using solid wood. Plywood is a good, inexpensive alternative. Several solid sheets of wood are glued together to manufacture plywood. It holds its shape well, and the layer of glue is much thinner in comparison to that used in particle board.

Tip: Even stubborn gnawers leave the box alone when delicious twigs and branches are part of the menu.

When turned over, module B becomes a delightfully fragrant bed full of hay for snuggling.

Construction Manual

How to Build Modules

The individual steps in building modules are not overly difficult. Since they are continually repeated, even less experienced woodworkers will soon get into the routine. Even if everything doesn't work out on the first try or is not 100% precise, you can be sure that the dwarfs won't object. Your first attempts are not necessarily a question of beauty. Above all, the safety of the inhabitants counts the most.

TOOLS	MATERIALS
□ Circular saw	□ Plywood pieces 12 inches wide, 3/4 inches thick (30 cm × 18 mm) for modules A and C
□ Jigsaw	
□ Cordless screwdriver	□ Plywood pieces, 12 inches (30 cm) and 15 3/4 inches (40 cm) wide, 3/4 inches (18 mm) for modules B, D, E, and F
□ Pilot drill, 1/8 inch (3 mm)	
□ Drill bit, 5/16 inch (8 mm) for countersinking and for wood dowels	
	□ 10–20 drywall screws 3/32 inch × 2 inch (4 mm × 50 mm) per module
□ Straightedge, compass, and pencil	□ As needed, wood dowels 1 1/4 inches (30 mm), 5/16 inch (8 mm), for assembly of multistory structures
□ Square	
□ Clamps	
□ Fine sandpaper or wood rasp	□ Small wood strips and nontoxic glue for module C

Cutting: The board is clamped to the workbench top and cut to the required dimensions with a circular saw. Some module types require a beveled cut so the boards can be joined at a specific angle (e.g., 45 degrees). For that purpose, the blade is simply adjusted to the angle and the cut is made as usual along the line drawn (photo 1).

Smoothing the edges: To keep the rabbits from injuring themselves on projecting or sharp edges, smooth all cut surfaces with sandpaper or a wood rasp (photo 2).

Assembly: All modules fasten together with screws. Use the small bit (1/8 inch /3 mm) to drill pilot holes that you can subsequently countersink with the large bit (5/16 inch/ 8 mm) so the screw heads will be flush with the surface. The structure will be stronger if you space out the screws evenly. Make sure that the top board always fits between the two side boards. That way, the tunnel will be slightly wider and the screws will not be on the surface where the rabbits walk (photo 3).

Tip: With uneven floors or very tall structures use more screws to connect the modules.

Openings: When making the openings, first make a cardboard template (diagram 1a, page 70) to save time. The distance from the center line of the opening to the right-hand

All the Steps at a Glance

Step 1: *Using the circular saw, cut out the boards along the lines drawn.*

Step 2: *Use a wood rasp or sandpaper to smooth the rough edges.*

Step 3: *Insert the screws into the slightly countersunk pilot holes.*

Step 4: *Draw the openings with the help of a template, and cut them out with a jigsaw.*

Step 5: *Wooden dowels will keep the modules from moving when they are stacked.*

Step 6: *Colorful paint or attractive decorations give the modules added visual appeal.*

edge of the module (or less commonly, to the left edge, from the builder's viewpoint) is always 6 9/16 inches/16.8 cm (diagram 1b, page 70). By sticking to this measurement, you can be sure that all the modules can be combined with one another without blocking off a passageway. When drawing the opening, leave a small, 1-inch (3 cm) crosspiece at the bottom. This will increase stability, serve as an attachment for a ramp, and make the module easier to handle. When you cut out the opening, first drill two pilot holes (5/16 inch/8 mm) near the corners so that the jigsaw can grab and turn effectively. Now cut out the opening very carefully (photo 4, page 19). You may have to tailor the size of the opening to your dwarf rabbits.

Tip: With many openings, the modules can be combined with one another in a variety of ways. If you intend to make a permanent structure, you can eliminate some openings, like in the rear wall. Instead, you can make the openings later if necessary.

Attaching the upper stories: Even though all the modules are compact and stable, they should be attached securely whenever two or more are installed above one another. Drill 5/16 inch (8 mm) vertical holes about ¾ inch (20 mm) deep in the long sidewalls of the lower module (approximately 2 inches/ 5 cm from the corner). Drill matching holes of the same diameter about 9/16 inch (15 mm) deep in the underside of the top module. Then install wood dowels in the holes in the

Tip

Use only safe materials and treat them with nontoxic paints and varnishes. Appropriate examples include linseed oil and varnish used on toys. When building the modules, make sure that no dangerous corners and edges stick out that could injure your dwarf rabbits. Regularly check the stability and workmanship of your structures to make sure they are safe.

lower module and simply place the upper module onto it. This connection is good insurance that the modules will stay in place and yet can be taken apart easily if necessary (photo 5, page 19).

Assembly and configuration: Even with just a few different types of modules, you can put together an attractive interior design for your dwarf rabbits. The possible variations are endless. A coat of beeswax will protect the wood and facilitate cleanup. Of course, you can also decorate the modules any way you want or give them a coat of an appropriate furniture paint. You may even want to draw or paint little works of art on the modules (photo 6, page 19).

Tip: For better traction, install some carpet remnants on the walking surfaces.

All the Module Types at a Glance

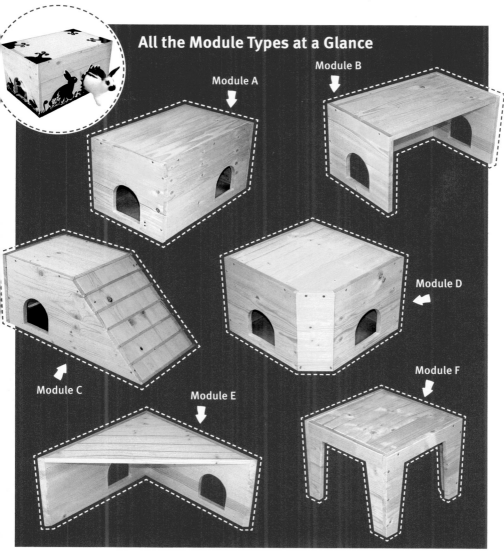

Module A

Module B

Module D

Module C

Module E

Module F

Module A: *The perfect beginner's model for a budding do-it-yourself enthusiast.*

Module B: *The open front makes it easy to integrate a litter box or a digging box.*

Module C: *A sturdy climbing wall with adequate traction.*

Module D: *This unit is easy to install in a corner.*

Module E: *This triangular model complements the basic types and provides visual variety.*

Module F: *The pavilion can serve as an individual element or complement the maze.*

Construction Manual

Module A: Tunnel Element

The tunnel element is a good basis for all modular structures. Even beginners in woodworking will find making this module within reach.

Step 1: Cut out 5 boards according to diagram 2a–b (page 70), and smooth the rough edges.

Step 2: Join two long boards lengthwise (photo 1).

Step 3: Attach the third long board to create a U shape (photo 2).

Step 4: Screw the small end pieces into place to create a box that is open underneath (photo 3).

Step 5: In the last step, make openings according to diagrams 1a and 1b (page 70) and smooth the rough edges.

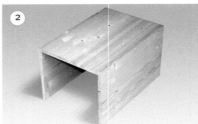

Construction Manual

Module B: Bridge Element

With its open front, the bridge element is best suited for making upper stories appear lighter and more casual.

Step 1: Cut out 4 boards according to diagrams 3a–3c (page 70), and smooth the rough edges.

Step 2: Screw a 12-inch (30 cm) board to a short one (photo 1).

Step 3: Screw the second short board into place (photo 2).

Step 4: Finish up by attaching the top board (photo 3).

Step 5: Make an opening in each of the narrow sidewalls according to diagrams 1a and 1b (page 70), and smooth the rough edges.

Module C: Ramp Element

To keep the inhabitants from slipping, cover the ramp with wood strips spaced at about 2-inch (5 cm) intervals or with carpet remnants after installing the sloped end.

Step 1: Cut out 5 boards according to diagrams 4a–d (page 71), and smooth the rough edges.

Step 2: Attach the 13¼ inch (33.6 cm) board to a trapezoid-shaped board (photo 1).

Step 3: Now screw the second trapezoid-shaped board and the top board into place (photo 2).

Step 4: Attach the board with the bevel cuts to the sloped area (photo 3).

Step 5: Make openings all the way around (except on the sloped side) according to diagrams 1a and 1b (page 70). With a trapezoid-shaped board, measure from the left.

Module D: Corner Element

With this module, you can build around a corner and create a decorative ending for a side or a projection on the front.

Step 1: Cut out 6 boards according to diagrams 5a–f (pages 71–72) and smooth the rough edges.

Step 2: Join both long boards with no bevel (photo 1).

Step 3: Bevel the boards on the right and the left (photo 2).

Step 4: Screw the top and front boards into place. Attach the front board to both side parts at the bottom (photo 3).

Step 5: Make openings in two sides as shown in diagrams 1a and 1b (page 70), and smooth the rough edges.

Module E: Additional Item 1

Construction Manual

This modular element with a triangular top surface is more than a complement to the basic modules. It also serves as a useful freestanding element.

Step 1: Cut out three boards according to diagrams 6a–c (page 72), and smooth the rough edges.

Step 2: First screw together the two rectangular sides (photo 1).

Step 3: Now screw the triangular top surface into place (photo 2).

Step 4: Make an opening according to diagrams 1a and 1b (page 70), and smooth the rough edges.

Note: In this case, the distance for the openings is measured from the left edge of the module (photo 3).

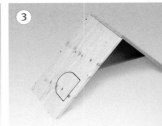

Module F: Additional Item 2 (Pavilion)

Construction Manual

A pavilion is a great addition to the maze (page 25). Make sure that the passageway is large enough if you modify the shape of the opening.

Step 1: Cut out 5 boards according to diagrams 7a–c (page 73), and smooth the rough edges.

Step 2: First join together two side boards of different sizes (photo 1).

Step 3: Now install the appropriate third board and the top board (photo 2).

Step 4: Finally, screw the remaining board into place (photo 3).

Step 5: Make openings all around according to diagram 8 (page 73), and smooth the rough edges. You can choose different shapes for the cutouts.

Top left: The dwarfs curiously follow the construction of their new play maze, which is very easy to assemble from modules A and E.

Top right: Adding module F is a perfect way to round out the maze. Wood dowels hold the pavilion in place.

Left: Pure digging fun. The step makes it easier to get into and out of; the cardboard wall serves as a splash guard.

Special Uses for Modules

Homemade modules are not just great for living. They can also be set up in countless ways.

Module A: The perfect digging paradise! Simply turn the module upside down and fill it with old dish towels or crumpled newspaper.

Module B: A bottom pan can be easily integrated into this module. Fill it with bedding, hay, or straw to turn it into a perfect cozy bed or a rabbit litter box. Cut down the sides of fairly deep pans to make it easier for the rabbits to go through.

Module C: If you put together two C modules front to front, they form a bridge with a passageway.

Module D: With no opening in place, turn it upside down and fill it with sand. You now have a ready-made digging box (photo at left).

Module E: Thanks to the beveled cuts, two E modules can be assembled into a rectangular module—a perfect hangout for dwarf rabbits.

Module F: In combination with modules A and E, this turns into a play maze in a jiffy. It invites the dwarfs to hide out, romp around, climb, and relax (photos above).

All-Purpose Modules

Whether as hideouts, sports arenas, cozy corners, adventure playgrounds, or a roomy living complex, modules can be set up in flexible configurations and can fit into every home. Modern rabbit furnishings can be designed individually and made to match the color scheme in the home perfectly. They also provide new accents with their exceptional design and fresh colors.

Goodbye, boredom. Because of the many construction possibilities, you can easily and continually put together a variety of new residential complexes for the dwarfs.

Like living in a fairy castle. The special design and the combination of modules gives this setup a special flair.

No place for a housing complex? No problem. With two modules, simply provide your dwarfs with a comfortable hiding place, a nice observation platform, and pure climbing fun. Even these modules offer several possible setups.

An original modular construction in Roman style. The dwarf rabbits love their atrium house. Its many passageways turn into a perfect home. The rabbits can romp around in the roomy front court or watch their companions' amusing antics from the observation platform.

Brisk traffic. The inhabitants can choose either an above- or a below-ground racetrack. They can even make a pit stop.

A nifty corner setup using just two module types. The roomy corner element offers a secure, cavelike hiding place. The carpet remnants glued in place provide good traction for dwarf rabbit feet.

Superstructure in black and white. If the floors are uneven, test the stability of the elements and screw them into place if necessary.

Modern chic with asymmetrical module setup and a variety of colors. The ramp is a board with slats glued in place; it is attached securely using hooks and eyes.

27

This is a great place to live. However, the rabbits still need to get out and run around on the floor every day.

Multistory Construction— Lots of Space in a Small Area

Dwarf rabbits like lots of room to move around. With a little imagination and a willingness to compromise, this can be accomplished even in a small area. If you don't have enough surface area, you can simply build vertically. Dwarf rabbits really like rooms with a view. Climbing to the upper stories helps keep them fit. With a ceiling height of 24 inches (60 cm), the dwarfs can sit up on their haunches and avoid hitting their heads

when they hop around. The ramps should not be too steep so that even elders can spend time on the upper floors. Take care to set up the levels in such a way that the rabbits have enough room for playing and hopping. Don't forget that rabbits are, by nature, ground creatures. Even though they live comfortably in a roomy multistory house, they need lots of chances to run around in order to work off their compulsion for exercise.

A Multistory Home

Building a multistory rabbit home requires a little skill. Use simple, ready-made wood shelving as a starting point. You can buy this type of shelving in various shapes and sizes. Our multistory home consists of two shelving units measuring 32 inches wide, 20 inches deep, and 70 inches tall (83 × 50 × 179 cm), each with four shelves, an appropriate corner post, and two corner shelves (30 inches wide × 30 inches deep × 20 inches tall (76 × 76 × 50 cm).

TOOLS

- □ Circular saw
- □ Jigsaw
- □ Drywall screws
- □ Hammer
- □ Tin snips
- □ 90° Square
- □ Spirit level
- □ Pencil and folding ruler for marking
- □ Staple gun
- □ 1/8 inch (3 mm) drill bit
- □ 5/16 inch (8 mm) drill bit
- □ Fine sandpaper for smoothing rough edges

MATERIALS

Note: Since the shelf measurements may vary, measure very carefully and adapt the specifications as needed before purchasing materials.

- □ Approx. 110 sq. ft. (10 m²) tongue-and-groove boards (4" [10 cm] overall width)
- □ 4 each flat-edge boards, 3¼" wide × ¾" thick (8 × 1.8 cm) in lengths of 20", 22", and 25 3/16" (51, 56, and 64 cm)
- □ Flat-edge boards, ¾" × 2" (1.8 × 5 cm) in the following lengths: 12 @ 28½" (72 cm), 2 @ 32" (81 cm), 5 @ 10" (25 cm), 2 @ 35½" (90 cm), 6 @ 31½" (80 cm)
- □ 2 pieces of plywood, 22" long × 9½" wide × ¾" thick (55 × 24 × 1.8 cm) and 18" long × 7 ¾" wide × ¾" thick (46 × 20 × 1.8 cm)
- □ 6 pieces of plywood, 24" long × 7¾" wide × ¾" thick (60 × 20 × 1.8 cm)
- □ About 13 linear feet (4 m) of 3-foot-wide (1 m) chicken wire with 1/16" (1.2 mm) wire and ¾" (20 × 20 mm) mesh
- □ 34 corner braces, 2" × 2" × 3/8" (5 × 5 × 1 cm)
- □ 1 package of staples, 5/16" (8 mm)
- □ Approx. 110 drywall screws, 5/32" × 1 ¼" (4 × 30 mm)

- □ Approx. 3,430 drywall screws, 5/32" × 2" (4 × 50 mm)
- □ 15 U-brackets, 3/8" × ¾" (10 x 20 mm): 12 pieces @ 2" (5 cm), 2 pieces at 18" (46 cm), and 1 piece at 7" (18 cm)
- □ 10 hooks and eyes for attaching ramps
- □ 6 small hooks
- □ 6 door hinges, one hinge 8" (20 cm) long, 1 window lock, wood handle
- □ Small wood strips and ¾" (20 mm) metal tacks for the ramps
- □ Nontoxic glue for the U-brackets

Let's see if our new house really is large enough.

Photo 1: Putting on the back and side walls.

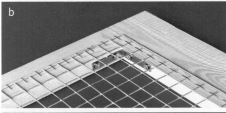

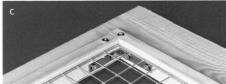

Photos 2a–c: Secure the doors with bite-proof wire.

Building and Decorating a Multistory Dwelling

Assemble the shelving units according to the manufacturer's instructions, and install the shelves as shown in photo 1. Now cover the back and side walls with untreated tongue-and-groove boards. Secure the boards into place horizontally. Use the frame of the shelving to provide secure attachment. Always push three boards together, hold them flush with one side, and mark the excess length on the other side. That way everything will fit when cut out. To secure the side walls, use 4 drywall screws per board. For the back, use 6 each (photo 1). When using screws, first drill a pilot hole with a 1/8 inch (3 mm) bit. Then countersink with a 5/16 inch (8 mm) bit so that the screw heads end up flush with the surface. Put the assembly into place, and adjust it with the spirit level. With young animals, you should close off the bottom so that the rabbits don't crawl under it when they are running around free.

Note: If there is a fairly large gap between the shelves and the wall when you cover the side walls, screw on a strip of wood of the right length and width to close it up. That way no rabbit will get hurt, and the bedding will stay where it belongs.

MAKING AND INSTALLING DOORS

Six small doors make it possible to access each story separately. Use flat-edge 2 inches × 3 inches (5 × 8 cm) boards to make two wood frames 34½ inches × 22 inches (88 ×

Photo 4: When the ramp is lowered, the dwarfs can find their own way out.

Photo 3: The ramp in closed position.

56 cm), 34½ inches × 20 inches (88 × 51 cm), and 34½ inches × 25 inches (88 × 64 cm) in size. The boards are butted up to one another and held together with small angle braces in the inside corners (photo 2a). Now cut out the chicken wire and staple it into place at short intervals (photo 2b). For safety, the edges of the wire can be covered with a strip of wood (photo 2c). This is necessary if you use so-called rabbit mesh instead of chicken mesh. The former is very unstable and may have sharp points and edges. The doors are attached to the corner posts of the shelves with hinges that swing open 180 degrees. This makes it easier to clean the rabbit house. Finally, install small hooks that latch into eyes (photo 3).

MIDDLE SECTION WITH EXIT

The front of the corner shelf consists of two wood frames, each of which is secured with 4 screws that can be removed quickly for major cleaning. The upper wood frame (32 inches × 13¾ inches [81 × 35 cm]), like the doors, is covered with mesh. At the level

of the second corner shelf, the lower frame (35½ inches × 13¾ inches [90 × 35 cm]) has an additional bridge that is covered with wire mesh at the bottom. The remaining

Photo 5: A pullout makes it easier to climb up.

Photo 2: Cutout for access to the upper story.

Photo 1: A view of how the shelves are set up.

Photo 3: Ramp attachment with hooks and eyes.

opening is closed with the larger piece of plywood in such a way that the board can be folded out and the inhabitants can use it as an exit ramp. Glue small wood strips into place to provide secure footing. Now glue three U-brackets (one 7 inches and two 18 inches long [18 cm and 46 cm]) in place so that the narrow piece of plywood can be slid in. Now the ramp can be extended at will to create a shallower climbing angle (photos 3–5, page 31). Grooves cut into the surface provide traction without interfering with the function.

Note: You may also want to secure the open front surface between the third and fourth corner shelves with wire mesh (photo 5, page 31). Older rabbits with impaired vision might otherwise take a fall.

Interior Accessories

Due to the special arrangement of the shelves, the dwarfs can romp on two continuous racecourses. The additional corner shelves extend the running surface (photo 1) and let the animals jump to the next floor. Six ramps guarantee that even the old and infirm can use all the levels. In addition, an 8 inch × 12 inch (20 × 30 cm) space is created on the right side of both rectangular shelves (1½ inches and 4 inches [4 and 10 cm] from the edges). This is easy to do with the jigsaw (photo 2, circle). First drill a 5/16 inch (8 mm) hole at each corner so that the saw can bite in and turn. Nail small wood strips onto the 8 inch × 24 inch (20 × 60 cm) ramp to improve security underfoot. The ramps are held in place with hooks and eyes so they can be easily removed if necessary (photo 3). To keep bedding from falling out when the door is opened, attach a 2 inch (5 cm) U-shaped bracket to the left and right doorposts. Slide in a smooth board measuring 2 inches × 31½ inches (80 × 5 cm), which you can easily remove for cleaning (photo 4).

SETUP AND ORGANIZATION

With animals that are not housebroken, you should apply a nontoxic varnish to the floors. Good choices are beeswax, linseed oil, and child-safe paint for toys. Apply several coats for adequate protection. Alternatively, you can also cover the floors with PVC to keep the rodent teeth from damaging them. Let new PVC air out first before installing it. Choose the furnishings carefully (photo, page 28). Cumbersome furniture that takes up lots of room is inappropriate for a multistory dwelling. Instead, make sure you include a private area for each dwarf, a digging box, and a pan with bedding. Including too many toys reduces the space for moving around. Additionally, you should replace them from time to time. Different floor structures on each level provide variety. Mats, tiles, and cork are possible choices, along with common bedding or a mixture of beneficial fresh leaves and dried greenery. Thick wooden plates are not only a neat decoration and a favorite material to gnaw—they also help keep the rabbits' nails and teeth short.

Tip: Attach several carrot holders (available at a pet shop) to the inside walls. You can put in fresh twigs or greens without interfering with the inhabitants' activities (photo, page 28).

Photo 4: The debris strip is easy to remove.

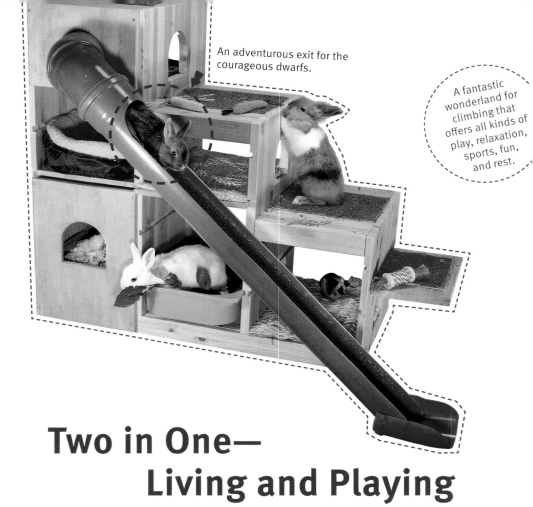

An adventurous exit for the courageous dwarfs.

A fantastic wonderland for climbing that offers all kinds of play, relaxation, sports, fun, and rest.

Two in One—
Living and Playing

If you have limited space for your dwarfs, you should put it to best use and set up the rabbit pen in the best way possible. Choose furnishings that combine multiple functions and are usable not just for living but also for games and activities. That way you will provide the dwarfs with entertainment and variety without reducing their available space. When you buy items, don't just fall for eye appeal. The right size, good workmanship, and material that can be gnawed are more important. Houses with pointed or domed roofs look neat to us. However, rabbits like elevated places with a good view, which only flat roofs can offer. Note which items your rabbits regularly use and enjoy. Remove furnishings that don't get used in order to create more space for hopping around.

Construction Manual

A Dwarf Rabbit Staircase

Practical, relatively easy to build, and far more than a boring, standard accessory—our clever dwarf rabbit staircase meets all these criteria. The basis of the staircase is a stepped shelf available in furniture stores. The adventurous dwarfs will take the new piece of furniture by storm. The more timid and the reluctant climbers may need a little time before they make their way to the top.

TOOLS

- Cordless screwdriver
- Jigsaw
- Circular saw
- Folding rule
- Pilot drill, 1/8 inch (3 mm)
- 5/16 inch (8 mm) drill bit for countersinking
- Pencil
- Compass
- Fine sandpaper

MATERIALS

- 1 stepped shelving unit measuring 37" high × 36" wide × 17" deep (94 × 91 × 44 cm)
- 6 shelves, 16½" × 12" (42 × 30 cm)
- 2 plastic tubs, 16½" × 12" × 4" (42 × 30 × 10 cm)
- 1 piece of plywood, 8" × 13¾" × 11/15" (20 × 35 × 1.8 cm)
- 2 metal brackets, 2¾" × 4¾" × 4" (7 × 12 × 10 cm)
- 16 drywall screws, 5/32" × 2" (4 × 50 mm)
- 1 PVC pipe, 5" (125 mm) diameter, 3 feet (1 m) long, with two 45° elbows and one 30° elbow
- One hinge 10" (25 cm) long with appropriate fasteners
- Nontoxic glue
- Carpet remnants

Step 1: Follow diagrams 9a-c (pp.73–74). Use the jigsaw to make openings in the inside walls of the individual elements and the lower outside wall. First drill two pilot holes right at the corners of the openings with the 5/16 inch (8 mm) bit so that the jigsaw can grab and turn. It's a lot easier to draw the openings if you prepare a template.
Step 2: Next make an opening in the bottom of one shelf according to diagram 10 (page 74).

Photo 1: Basic construction of the stepped-shelf frame.

Step 3: Use the circular saw to cut out a shelf measuring 8½ inch × 12 inch (22 × 30 cm) and a circular opening according to diagram 11 (page 74).

Step 4: Smooth all sawed edges using fine sandpaper.

Step 5: Now put together the shelving according to the manufacturer's instructions. Install three untreated shelves in such a way that the dwarf rabbits can hop through the openings in the walls of the shelving and into the next space. Put the plastic tubs into the lowest floor. Later they will be filled with bedding, hay, stray, or sand to serve as nests for snuggling, a digging box, or a litter box (photo page 35).

Step 6: Use the hinge to attach the last untreated shelf board to the bottom shelf of the tallest section. When the board is lifted, it can be pushed back a bit into the groove with the other shelf. That way the board holds securely, allowing you to take out the

Tip

Not every rabbit owner is a gifted do-it-yourselfer. Still, your dwarfs needn't be deprived of a totally original setup. Look for everyday items that can be remodeled without too much trouble. A stocking can be turned into a fun hay dispenser. An old sweater can become a comfortable cuddling place. A discarded table can be converted into a shelter with a few flicks of the wrist.

plastic tub easily for cleaning. The hatch can also be used as a little veranda or a springboard (photos 2 and 3).

Photo 2: Install the front board with a hinge.

Photo 3: The open hatch allows easy tub removal.

Photo 5: Installation of the slide made from PVC pipe and the appropriate elbows.

Photo 4: Screwing the shelves into place.

Step 7: Secure both shelves to the shelving frame as shown in photo 4. Insert 4 screws at a slight angle at each corner. Drill a pilot hole with the 1/8 inch (3 mm) bit, and countersink with the 5/16 inch (8 mm) bit to a depth where the screw heads are flush with the surface.

Step 8: In this step, insert a 45° PVC elbow into the round top opening from the inside. Then push the second 45° elbow onto it firmly.

Step 9: Use the jigsaw to cut the PVC pipe and the 30° elbow lengthwise far enough for the rabbits to walk up and down easily. Smooth the rough edges on both pieces, and put the pieces together (photo 5).

Step 10: Since the first step in the staircase is fairly high, add a small additional step. A piece of plywood is used for this. Screw it in place with the two corner braces at a height of approximately 9 inches (23 cm) (photo 6).

Step 11: For increased security underfoot, cover the pipe ramp and the stairs with carpet remnants (photo, page 34).

Step 12: Done! After you put away the tools and materials, you can open the staircase to the herd of dwarfs for their investigation. Which rabbit will be the first one to climb to lofty heights and enjoy the view?

Note: Don't place the staircase right next to a fence for the pen. Otherwise it may be used as a springboard into forbidden pastures.

Photo 6: Securing the footboard with corner braces.

Versatile Furnishings with Pizzazz

Furnishings that can be used for a variety of activities are just what the bubbly, cheeky dwarfs want. This guarantees that they will not become bored. Whether for hiding games or a siesta—everyone will find their favorite pieces. In addition, furnishings often give the dwarfs a pedicure and act as an abrasive for the teeth. Sometimes the *tasteful* furnishings may also get eaten.

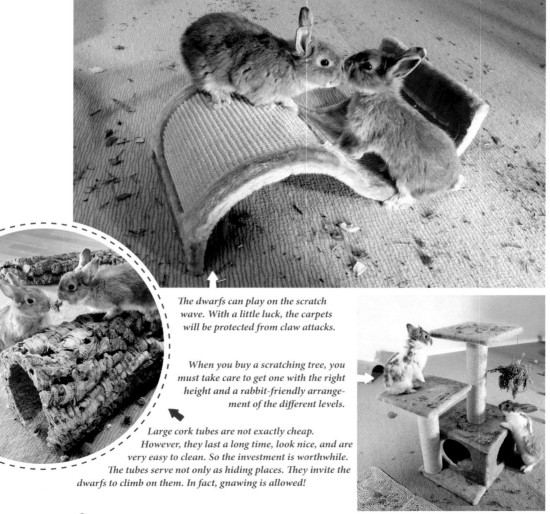

The dwarfs can play on the scratch wave. With a little luck, the carpets will be protected from claw attacks.

When you buy a scratching tree, you must take care to get one with the right height and a rabbit-friendly arrangement of the different levels.

Large cork tubes are not exactly cheap. However, they last a long time, look nice, and are very easy to clean. So the investment is worthwhile. The tubes serve not only as hiding places. They invite the dwarfs to climb on them. In fact, gnawing is allowed!

A perfect panoramic view. Houses with flat roofs are not only comfortable hideouts but also lookout points that the dwarfs really love and can reach in a hop. They are a great spot for taking a close look at the surroundings.

A wicker tunnel is a fun hideout and a place to catch some winks. Unfortunately, sometimes a buddy comes by and gives the tunnel a good jiggle.

Grass tubes come in a variety of sizes so that even chubby dwarfs can scamper through them. When the dwarfs have had their fill of playing with the tasty tunnel, it gets eaten up with gusto.

Custom tunnels can be made from carpet remnants. Just roll them to the desired diameter and hold them together with a cord.

This homemade bridge incorporates a variety of materials to provide different surfaces for the paws. The various floor structures help keep the claws worn down and eliminate the need for tedious pedicures.

JUICY GREEN GRASS IS THE FAVORITE
FOOD OF ALL RABBITS.

Outdoors—
Lots of Freedom

Even if the indoor villa is set up to be an exciting place, rabbits
need to get outdoors to experience lots of freedom: scampering
through the yard, digging to their hearts' content, and experiencing
all the seasons. A dwarf doesn't need much more to be happy.

Flush-mounted wire mesh prevents breakouts and intrusions.

A well-designed and well-constructed, large outdoor pen is an oasis of well-being for the dwarfs.

Considerations for Outdoor Living

The outdoors contains many stimulating scents and sounds, all kinds of room to romp around, and a thousand mysterious corners that demand exploration. Outdoor housing is perfect happiness for dwarfs. The outdoor time stimulates the creatures' senses. The dwarfs commonly surprise their owner with totally new behaviors. The expanded sphere of action has a positive effect on digestion, keeps the musculoskeletal system fit, and prevents respiratory problems. Healthy materials for gnawing are good for teeth and

gums. A variety of ground structures prevents you from having to do tedious nail trimming. However, outdoor housing comes with a price. It's a lot more time consuming than indoor accommodations and it involves higher expenses. The most important additional requirements for the dwarfs are safety and protection from the weather.

Total security: With rabbits we must think of three main directions: over, under, and through. Housing made from bite-resistant, tight wire mesh on all sides makes sure that no enemy can get in and that no dwarf can make a run for it. Alternatively, the ground beneath can be secured with concrete slabs or with the same flush-mounted wire mesh that's used on the sides.

Warm and protected: The location for the rabbit cottage must be protected from wind and weather. For 3 to 4 rabbits, 10 square feet (1 m²) of interior space will suffice. The cottage is heated solely by the animals' body heat. It must be built of strong wood at least ¾ inch (2 cm) thick or double-walled and insulated with Styrofoam. Holes drilled in the upper part provide for adequate ventilation. A partition in the entrance protects against draft. Line the cottage with ample hay and straw. In combination with a generous area to run around in and get warm, the dwarfs can even withstand severe winters.

THE RIGHT TYPE OF PEN

With pens that cover a small surface area, you should provide an outside shelter so you don't reduce the area where the animals can run around.

Flat pen: This is a good choice for small yards. The costs for construction and maintenance are manageable. The design options and the construction of upper

stories and raised platforms are necessarily restricted. The reduced size means that setup, care, and cleaning are often difficult despite having hinged roofs.

Tip: Pens from a pet shop usually are suitable for only short stays outdoors, but they can be upgraded. Just make sure they cover an area of at least 43 square feet (4 m²) for two inhabitants, include a well-insulated shelter hut, and provide good ground protection (top photo below).

Walk-in pens: This type of pen requires lots of space. However, the large sphere of action allows for a good floor plan and the inclusion of many levels. A person can stand upright inside the pen, making all tasks easier. Construction and maintenance are cost intensive. Because of the size and the permanence of the installation, a local building permit may be required.

Top: A winter-proof combination of two outdoor pens from a pet shop.
Far left: A walk-in rectangular pen near the house.
Left: A walk-in, wedge-shaped pen with entrances on both ends and partial roofing.

43

Glued-on cork sheets reduce the danger of slipping.

Walking across the slightly wobbly suspension bridge requires courage and skill and is not for scaredy-cats.

Some Clever Setups

A cleverly designed outdoor pen is not merely an ideal paradise for the dwarfs but also a real highlight in your yard. Use as many natural materials as possible when you set it up. They look good in all outdoor pens, stand up to wind and weather, and are real favorites with the rabbits. Choose materials based on functionality, safety, and ease in cleaning. Avoid reducing the surface area inside the pen with objects that may look good but are impractical. Often it's the

simple things that brighten rabbit hearts. Regularly reorganizing the setup provides variety for the dwarfs. Often the inhabitants themselves rearrange their home. The rabbits dig, turn things upside-down, and shove everything movable back and forth. Don't attempt to go back to the old arrangement. The dwarfs will tirelessly show their talents as master builders. Accept their lifestyle, and spare yourself lots of work and stress.

Suspension Bridge

Construction Manual

Would you like to provide your protégés with an original, functional accessory even though you don't have the necessary skills to build it? The next time you are out shopping, take a tour of discovery to find objects that can be easily remodeled into neat rabbit furnishings.

TO MAKE A SUSPENSION BRIDGE, YOU WILL NEED THE FOLLOWING:

2 step stools 18″ × 15″ × 18″ (45 × 39 × 48 cm); linked rolled fencing approx. 12″ wide × 43″ long (30 × 110 cm);

4 pieces of plywood 18″ × 8″ × ¾″ (45 × 20 × 1.8 cm); 2 laths 16″ × 8″ × 72″ (40 × 20 × 180 cm); 4 each hooks and eyes;

16 drywall screws 5/32″ × 2″ (4 × 50 mm); circular saw and jigsaw; screwdriver; drill; sandpaper

---

Step 1: Assemble the step stool (purchased from a furniture store or building supplies store) without installing the board for the first step.

Step 2: Cut the 4 pieces of plywood with the circular saw according to diagram 12 (page 74), and smooth the edges with sandpaper. Install 2 of them where the first step should be (photo 1).

Step 3: Attach the boards with 4 screws each. Drill a pilot hole with the 1/8 inch (3 mm) bit, then countersink the holes with the larger bit so the screw heads are flush with the surface (photo 2).

Step 4: Install 2 eyes on the top step and 2 matching hooks on the rolled fencing (photo 3).

Step 5: Suspend the rolled fencing between the two step stools, and line up the hanging bridge. Now screw two wood slats of the appropriate length to the outer edges of the step stool legs (left photo) so that nothing tips when overweight or overexuberant dwarfs use the suspension bridge. Drill pilot holes, and countersink the screws.

Step 6: The bridge will last for a long time if you apply a good coat of exterior paint.

Note: With step stools that have a cut-out hand hold, close up the opening so no rabbit can get hurt.

Stairs and Ramps

You can build additional levels inside a high-walled pen. They not only increase the rabbit's sphere of activity but also provide coveted observation platforms. Make sure that all animals can get into the weatherproof shelter easily. If the ramps are placed at an incline of 30 to 35 degrees, even seniors and patients with restricted mobility will be able to use them. However, you should also provide your dwarfs with more demanding stairs and gradients. They encourage fitness, nimbleness, and balance. The following rules basically apply to all ramps: not too narrow, not too steep, and always securely attached. Regularly check all ramps and their load-bearing capacity. Secure all attachments. Make sure the area underfoot is safe. Outdoors the wind and weather leave their mark. A coat of nontoxic paint will protect against premature weathering. Additionally, do not underestimate the continuous damage caused by eager rodent teeth.

The classics: The simplest solution to provide secure access is wood ramps (photo 3). You can contribute to surefootedness by gluing, screwing, or nailing small wood strips or by cutting in some grooves. The latter is easiest with a circular saw. Alternatively, you can find in pet shops ready-made ramps with the requisite grooves (photo 2).

Step by step: Dwarf rabbits are very fond of stairs. The steps can be made of wood (photo 1), or you can stack concrete blocks and bricks to form a stable staircase. The dwarfs will take every staircase by storm.

At a hop: You can provide the jocks among your dwarfs with a variety of elevated observation platforms (photo 4). These platforms provide a great view and allow jumping to the upper levels. Cork sheets tacked onto slippery surfaces prevent slipping.

On the steep trail: An imaginative but functional ramp can be made from a large roof gutter (photo 5). Use tin snips to cut a loop out of one side, and bend it to the rear at an appropriate angle. Then secure the gutter to the floorboard with 2 screws. Carpet remnants glued in place will give rabbit paws the necessary traction.

Here going up and down turns into a bold climbing feat. This is not for dwarfs with impaired mobility.

1 An open staircase made from wood is a quick project. Just make sure that it's solidly constructed. Angle braces screwed in underneath provide adequate security. The height, length, and width of the steps should be adapted to your dwarfs. Jocks will take two steps at a time.

2 Two ramps from the pet shop placed side by side. These can be lengthened and widened by adding more ramps. The treated walking surface helps wear down the dwarfs' toenails.

3 The dwarfs will conquer any height by climbing wood ramps. Small wood strips nailed in place reduce the risk of slippage. This provides the ideal access to elevated shelters.

4 An alternative to ramps and the like: old flowerpot stands in appropriate heights can be shortened and covered with sheets of cork.

5 Exceptional access: a gutter provides security even for scaredy-cats. The carpet remnants glued in place provide traction for the dwarfs' toenails.

Furnishings with a Natural Flair

What could be more appropriate in an outdoor pen than furnishings made from natural materials? They will not only delight the dwarfs but will also stand up against wind and weather. You can usually get them for practically nothing. On your next walk in the woods, you will surely find an attractive root or a forked branch. You can also find neat things in pet shops and building supply stores that can be used for an imaginative and natural pen design.

You can buy wire-bound, rolled fencing for garden beds. Set it up in a spiral pattern to make a neat maze for curious dwarf rabbits.

This small animal house offers a roomy shelter and a roof terrace with a great view.

Constructed in the twinkle of an eye is a cozy, wedge-shaped shelter made from four coarse cork sheets. A lath under the ridge increases stability. The tile underlay provides comfortable cooling in the summer. In the winter, a wood insert protects against dampness and cold.

The cool spots inside earthen tunnels are very popular on hot summer days. A connecting PVC pipe (at right in the photo) serves as an emergency exit. After relaxing, the dwarfs can have a little climbing excursion on the reinforced stone mountain.

A neat adventure playground with the feeling of a real cave. The dwarfs scamper through it, climb on it, laze in the sun, and go inside for a little nap.

The idyllic watering hole in the shade of a deciduous tree has become a really comfortable oasis for our rabbits. It invites them to refresh themselves and linger for a while.

A forked stick with burlap bags stretched over it quickly creates a tepee. The tent also resists a rain shower.

When painted, modules from indoors work fine in the yard. Additional holes provide adequate ventilation in the summer.

STANDING ON ITS HAUNCHES GIVES EVEN THE TINIEST DWARF A GOOD VIEW.

Games, Sports, and All Kinds of Fun

A green light for the great games and sports program: with the right activities, your dwarf rabbits will experience new and exciting adventures every day. Boredom and idleness will have no chance.

Metal rings and spring hooks allow you to adjust the height quickly.

A great spot for sleeping and relaxing. A hammock will not go unused for very long.

Top Choices for Rabbits That Can Entertain Themselves

No owner can be available to the rabbits around the clock. Long-term supervision is also not necessary because the dwarfs are good at keeping themselves occupied. However, dwarfs always need mental and physical activities. Pet shops offer a colorful assortment of appropriate toys. However, you can also stimulate the rabbits' curiosity and satisfy their urge to discover with homemade items. This also contributes to fitness and health. Not every toy will be accepted enthusiastically

right away. Sometimes it takes days for some meddlesome dwarf to investigate the new item. Then the toy may turn into a long-term favorite and bring a new impetus into the rabbits' daily routine. The item may, instead, fall flat in the test run and remain ignored in a corner. When the rabbits are kept outdoors, romping around is at the top of the list of free-time activities. An extensive race course is second only to a big digging box in which the rabbits can satisfy their passion for tunneling.

Construction Manual

Reversible Hammock

Dwarf rabbits are very active and bubbly, but they still enjoy their rest breaks. What could be better than hanging out in a comfortable spot? A hammock is just the right thing. Making one is no great feat. If you don't like to sew, you can simply adapt a small face towel.

YOU WILL NEED THE FOLLOWING TO MAKE A REVERSIBLE HAMMOCK:
Tear-proof fabric in two different patterns; paper for a template; a ruler and a pencil for drawing; pins; scissors; sewing machine; needles and thread; 8 metal sewing eyelets approx. 5/16 inch (8 mm) in diameter; an eyelet plier; several metal rings; 4 spring hooks

Step 1: Cut a sheet of newspaper to 22 inch × 16 inch (55 × 40 cm). Cut off each corner about 3 inches (8 cm) from the edge. Attach this pattern with pins to 2 pieces of fabric, each with a different design. Cut out the 2 pieces of cloth (photo 1). You should create a winter and a summer side, that is, a combination of cooling and warming materials such as linen and fleece. Both fabrics should be machine washable.

Note: Always prewash new fabric before cutting it.

Step 2: Place the pieces of fabric on top of one another with the right sides facing in, and sew them together up to one corner.

Step 3: Turn the piece inside out. Slightly turn in the edge on the still-open side, and sew the fabric together.

Step 4: Draw the locations for the round metal eyes on the corners about 1 inch (3 cm) from the edge. Use the eyelet pliers to fasten 8 metal sewing eyelets (photo 2).

Step 5: Insert a metal ring through adjacent eyelets. You can put in more rings depending on the possibilities for hanging the hammock. Attach a spring hook to each of the 4 metal rings so the hammock can be hung securely anywhere (photo 3).

Solo Games and Snuggle Spots

Interesting and tricky solo games make great pastimes for rabbits. You can find a broad selection in pet shops. Caves have a magical attraction for dwarfs. Tunnels and pipes are right at the top of the hit list. Even paw games are received enthusiastically. The rabbits love to roll, push, and kick things tirelessly. After the wild play sessions, comfy places beckon them to relax.

Whether from the pet shop or homemade, snuggle sacks are the absolute blockbusters among dwarf rabbits. The extra large size provides enough room for two.

Tunnels and pipes are hotly sought after, and caves exert a magical attraction on dwarf rabbits. Several exits make for perfect bliss.

"Casanova" loves to pounce on anything made of paper. Old telephone books are his favorite shredding material. He zealously rips the pages into little strips and spreads them all around the room. Maybe you too have a little shredder among your dwarfs.

A real feat of strength. Wicker and wood barbells encourage biting. They are also great for flinging around or can be pushed across the whole pen with a powerful kick. Better keep your head down because there is always a possibility of a glancing shot.

Not just for the cat: Rabbits too like the comfort of a couch that can be attached to a wall or hung on a radiator. The elevated location provides a good view.

Colorful wicker balls provide the hoppers with long-term fun. The bell inside them provides musical entertainment with every kick.

A digging paradise for dwarf rabbits. Select only materials in which the animals' claws will not get caught.

A grass bed from the pet shop. It's a tight fit with double occupancy. However, no dwarf will voluntarily give up the cozy spot, which may also soon be eagerly gobbled up.

Quick and Easy— A Cardboard City

You can easily build neat and inexpensive hiding places from sturdy cardboard boxes and tubes. You can even make whole cardboard cities. Naturally, the structures are not intended to last forever. When the dwarfs have played with them enough, they will pull the cardboard houses into their component parts and gnaw on them. So use only plain cardboard. If you want colors, decorate them with nontoxic paint.

Whether a knight's castle, a fairy palace, or a modern apartment complex—the possibilities for a cardboard city are without limit.

The basic materials for the cardboard houses are sturdy cartons, tubes, and packing materials in all shapes and sizes.

First determine what you want to build. Then draw the necessary openings. Using a template will make the job easier. The openings must be adapted to the size of the dwarfs. Cut out the openings with scissors or a box cutter. Be careful. Children can easily hurt themselves.

56

Sturdy cardboard tubes are great for making pillars. Cut both ends evenly at several places. Fold the resulting flaps outward. Stick the tubes to the floor and roof plates of the structure with double-sided tape.

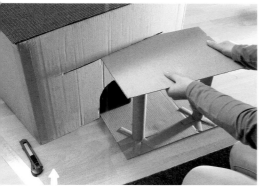

Two columns are adequate for porch roofs and balconies. Cut a slit into the box at the appropriate height, and slide the roof plate into place. Then attach the floor plate under the box.

The openings for connecting tunnels should be cut out for the best fit possible. Sliding them into larger boxes adds stability.

Cut out battlements and other embellishments for the dwarf castle, and attach them with double-sided tape.

Cover running surfaces with carpet remnants. This gives the cardboard city extra eye appeal and provides better traction for rabbit feet.

A colorful array of vegetables provides the dwarfs with important vitamins.

The food wheel attracts rabbits with its delicious treats. Which of the rabbits will be the first to figure out the trick?

Food Games That Increase Fitness

Many rabbits that are kept as pets tend to become overweight. Their wild relatives have to search arduously for their food every day, but our pets enjoy a sumptuous table setting. Foods high in calories and too little exercise cause the bunny that was once slender and bursting with life to turn into a lazy, fat pudge. Try to prevent this, because excess weight is bad for the dwarfs' health. Provide healthy, well-balanced food. Give small treats in moderation. However, calorie bombs should be the exception. You can use amusing food games to inspire the rabbits to exercise more and simultaneously encourage dexterity, cleverness, and physical fitness. Don't forget the loafers and couch potatoes. They too need their regular food ration, especially hay. The rabbits' favorite food must always be available to them, preferably in easily reachable racks. You must never subject your rabbits to fasting; doing so could be life threatening.

58

Food Wheel

You can build a food wheel in the twinkle of an eye. You don't need to make anything special. You can use common, everyday items for most of the components. Which of the dwarfs is clever enough to figure out the spinning action and get the tasty treats first?

YOU WILL NEED THE FOLLOWING TO MAKE A FOOD WHEEL:
1 revolving wood platter about 15″ (39 cm) in diameter; 1 wood dowel 2 feet (60 cm) long; 8 sharpened 3/8 inch (10 mm) wood dowels 4 inch (10 cm) long; 1 Christmas tree stand; a cordless drill; a hammer; a saw; 1/8 inch, 5/16 inch, and 3/8 inch (3, 8, and 9 mm) drill bits; a folding ruler; pencil sharpener; pencil for drawing; two 5/32 × 2 inch (4 × 50 mm) drywall screws

---

Step 1: On the wood platter (available from household supply stores) make eight marks similar to the face of a clock 1 3/16″ (3 cm) from the edge. Drill holes with the 3/8″ (10 mm) bit.

Step 2: Firmly drive in the sharpened dowels with a hammer (photo 1).

Step 3: Drill 6 holes 2″ (5 cm) apart in the 2 foot (60 cm) wood dowel. Use the 1/8″ (3 mm) bit for the pilot hole and the 5/16″ (8 mm) as a countersink so that the screw heads will sit flush.

Step 4: Drill two holes into the centerline of the small disk on the back of the wood platter. They should be 2″ (5 cm) from the pivot point.

Step 5: Attach the shaft to the plate with 2 screws. Use the additional holes to adjust the height (photo 2).

Step 6: Secure the wood shaft in the Christmas tree stand, put some treats onto the food wheel, and get ready for the test run (photo 3).

Tip: For outdoor use, you can simply fashion a point on the shaft and drive it into the ground.

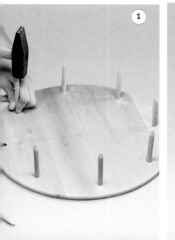

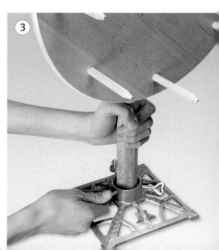

The Tastiest Food Games

Food games are lots of fun, and they use up accumulated calories. Traditional items such as hay bales, skewered vegetables, and food ropes that you can make yourself are very inexpensive. Pet shops offer more options—from simple carrot holders to tricky snack balls and the heavenly food tree. Homemade items provide additional variety and encouragement.

In order to make the homemade seesaw more attractive to little scaredy-cats, it was upgraded with a wood frame that attracts rabbits with lots of treats. Nibbling a carrot is a real challenge due to the continual up and down motion.

Spiced-up classic: thread cardboard tubes onto a string, fill them with hay, and hang them up. In this case, feeding becomes a game of agility.

Dwarfs really like snack balls. A little surprise falls out every time it is kicked.

The homemade food carousel must be well assembled because the dwarfs really have to work hard in order to eat. If a buddy joins the buffet, things become doubly difficult. When the dwarf thinks it has a treat, presto—the carousel turns and the dwarf ends up empty-handed.

A quick meal on wheels. Patience and agility are required with the vegetable roller since it never stands still. Saucy dwarfs simply swipe from a successful buddy.

This mesh ball hung up inside the pen is well stocked with treats. Lots of endurance and skill are needed to grab the treats in the swinging food dispenser.

Screw two laminated boards into a T shape, and drill some holes. The food wall is now done!

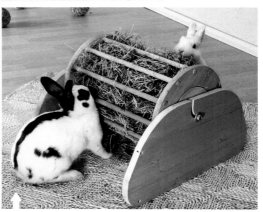

The hay dispenser can also be set up as a free-moving roller or with the container held immobile. An opening on the side makes it quick and easy to fill with hay.

61

The ropes require the use of the teeth.

Heave-ho: the goal is reachable with cleverness, skill, and endurance.

Solving Puzzles with Skill and Gumption

Anyone who thinks that rabbits are dumb is gravely mistaken. The little fellows are very crafty and can surprise us with unimagined skills. In the wild, cleverness and an aptitude for learning are important weapons in the daily struggle for survival. No wonder that many dwarfs show themselves to be real masterminds in intelligence games. They puzzle over things as long as it takes to get the reward treat. Others lurk around the bizarre thing and examine everything closely without doing anything about it. This doesn't necessarily have anything to do with lack of interest. These dwarfs are thinkers, who first observe their colleagues and learn from their failed attempts. Then at some time, the thinkers come by and solve the problem in nothing flat. However, don't fret if a dwarf wants nothing to do with intelligence games. Maybe it prefers to run or climb rather than deal with unwieldy games of wit.

Intelligence Games and Games of Wit

Intelligence games test the cleverness of your dwarfs. Games of wit are a perfect way for the rabbits to entertain themselves because they foster both skill and gumption. If your rabbits get deeply involved in a game and have fun, it has served its purpose—regardless of whether the task was accomplished immediately, eventually, or never. Here's how to get your dwarfs started right.

No time restrictions: Let the little brain acrobats puzzle things out as long as they want. Your dwarf rabbits should always have the chance to solve the task at hand themselves—even if it takes a couple of days or longer.

Motivational aids: If a dwarf is on the right track but is struggling for a fairly long time with the opening mechanism, give it a treat as a reward for ambition and persistence. The treat keeps a dwarf happy and motivates it to keep working at the game.

Get them started right: Sometimes dwarfs fall short of success even after stubbornly trying. Then you should provide assistance by showing a glimpse of the food reward or by demonstrating how the game works several times in succession. Rabbits are attentive observers and learn very quickly.

Something new: Make several intelligence games available. We often misjudge the level of difficulty. Often a dwarf falls short on a simple game but masters a presumably much harder test with flying colors.

Shortcut: There is no single shortcut for the games are too varied in the way they work. The principle is simple. Anything that works counts as a success. With interested dwarfs, we can identify a type of pattern in problem solving. Generally, the game is first inspected and the hidden treat is sniffed out (photo 1). Now the dwarf employs its nose and head to clear away the obstacle (photo 2). If that doesn't work, usually the next step involves striking the object with the paws (photo 3). Often using the teeth leads to success (photo on opposite page).

Tricky Intelligence Games

Intelligence games work in various ways and continually pose new challenges for the dwarfs. Some can be particularly difficult. Cunning brain acrobats can solve demanding games intended for dogs and cats.

However, pay attention to the materials and workmanship of the games. Some games won't stand up to rabbit teeth for very long and should be used only under supervision.

Whether to bite and pull out or to hit it with the paw is the question. Every dwarf will develop its own technique to get at the hidden treat.

The ball game requires the use of mainly the nose and head. It is also a good game for dwarfs with dental problems.

This is a game made for dogs, but many dwarfs can undertake it with the sophistication of the barking faction. In order to get to the treats, the dwarfs must shove aside the movable pieces with the nose or paws. Clever dwarfs soon get the hang of it.

This is a homemade intelligence game. When the pivoting food container is turned upside down, little treats tumble out of the opening in the top. A weight in the bottom continually returns the container to the starting position, and that complicates the task.

Here the dwarf needs a good nose and lots of skill because the treats are hidden underneath hatches. The special difficulty is that the hatches open on different sides.

This is a really sticky wicket. The treats look like they are easily within reach. In order to get at them, though, the rabbit must first pull out the drawer.

Stockpiles in drawers: when the bottom drawer is pulled out, the next one slides down and becomes accessible.

This is a wood block with little depressions for hiding treats. There are knobs on the lids. If the dwarfs grip the knobs with their teeth, they can take off the covers.

65

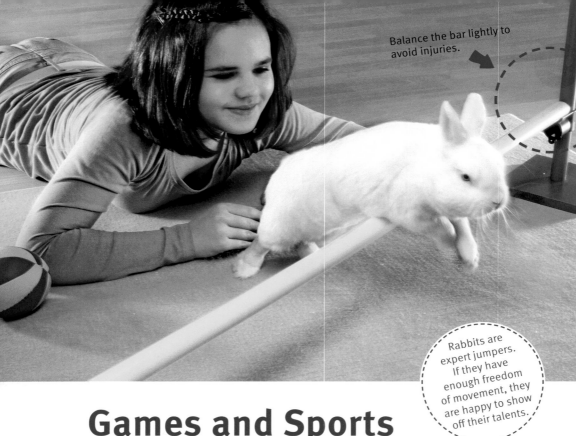

Balance the bar lightly to avoid injuries.

Rabbits are expert jumpers. If they have enough freedom of movement, they are happy to show off their talents.

Games and Sports with Humans

Absolute trust in the owner is the prerequisite for having fun together. Only an anxiety-free animal will get completely involved with humans, play with them, and consider their mock attacks as what they really are: harmless and fun. With dwarf rabbits, love is a matter of the stomach. You can win their trust quickly by feeding them their favorite foods. At first, the dwarfs will only snatch the treats and go back into hiding. Later on, they will even eat from your hand. Start with simple games as soon as the rabbits appear to be totally at ease in your presence, and initiate physical contact. At first, avoid frantic movements so you don't frighten the animals. Eventually, even fairly rough-and-tumble games will work. Reconcile yourself to the fact that a human often looks rather old in comparison to the agile bunnies. Not every dwarf likes this type of game. Accept the situation if the rabbits prefer the company of their colleagues.

Rabbit Jumping Without a Leash

Rabbit jumping provides all kinds of exercise and fun. The dwarfs can do without the stress of competition. If they enjoy jumping over the hurdles, you will need no leash or harness. Find out if your little rascals are ready for rabbit jumping. You may have a highly gifted rabbit jumper among your dwarfs.

MATERIALS
A hurdle with adjustable height and a loosely balanced bar

Step 1: Place the hurdle onto a soft surface to protect the animal's joints. Start with low jumps and a bar height of no more than 2 inches (5 cm).

Step 2: Lead the dwarf to the obstacle with little vegetable treats. A special treat on the other side of the hurdle provides the necessary motivation for the jump (photo 1).

Step 3: This rarely works the first time. The crafty dwarfs simply run around the hurdle, and the lazy ones ignore the treat. The best solution is to repeat the attempt in short sessions. For every successful jump over the hurdle, praise the rabbit and give it a little reward.

Step 4: If a dwarf doesn't understand how this works, carefully lift it over the hurdle—but only if the animal trusts you and does not panic the moment it loses contact with the floor.

Step 5: Once the game sinks in and the dwarf enjoys jumping, it will go over the hurdle even without assistance (photo 2). Eventually, you can raise the bar and set up several hurdles in succession. However, don't demand too much from your brigade!

Note: If a dwarf shows absolutely no ambition for jumping, it will surely find other games to be more fun.

Unlimited Fun

Sports and games have no limits. Whatever is fun and always safe for the rabbits is fair game. Make use of the creatures' active phases and play then. They will be in a good mood and ready for practically any kind of fun. Every shared activity strengthens the basis of trust between you and your protégés. After the strenuous exercise program, the dwarfs should take a good rest.

Set up a couple of obstacles, and lure your rabbit through the slalom course with a treat. After several training runs, the treat should come only at the end. Will the dwarf learn the course, or will it take the shortest route?

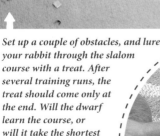

Bowling without a ball: your dwarfs will be happy to clean up. As soon as the pins are set up, the fur balls will dash into them again and knock everything over.

Rolling along nicely: choose a ball of the right size so that your dwarf doesn't feel bowled over.

Some dwarfs are real climbers, and no mountain is too high for them. There is nothing wrong with making yourself available as a climbing object. This will strengthen the relationship with your protégés. Be aware that you may very probably be scratched.

Using a homemade fishing pole with a treat for bait is a fun game. Hold the rod in such a way that the dwarfs have to strain and stretch diligently.

Taking a Break After Playing

Dwarfs can get out of breath from cavorting around with the owner and will need to take an occasional break—whether long or short. Of course, it's fine to let the play session die down together (photo below). However, you should also accept it if some of your little playmates prefer to pull back and relax in their hiding places.

Encouraging Play

The best encouragement for every game is always a juicy treat. However, don't tease the dwarf rabbits too much by always moving the treat beyond their reach. Otherwise, your playmates will quickly lose interest. Small successes will keep up their spirits. For scaredy-cats that are too timid to take food from their owner's hand, distance games such as the vegetable pole (photo above) are a good choice. Start with a long pole, and shorten it gradually. This is one way to build your protégés' trust.

Some dwarfs are glad to be coddled and petted. Find out what your pet enjoys. Is it a delicate massage or a gentle brushing?

Diagrams for the Modular Structures, pages 22–24

Diagram 1a—Pattern

5" (13 cm)

5" (13 cm)

Diagram 1b—Location of Opening

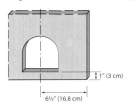

1" (3 cm)

6½" (16.8 cm)

Diagram 2a—Module A

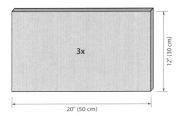

3x

12" (30 cm)

20" (50 cm)

Diagram 2b—Module A

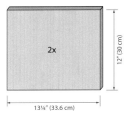

2x

12" (30 cm)

13¼" (33.6 cm)

Diagram 3a—Module B

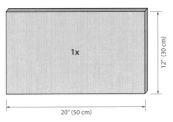

1x

12" (30 cm)

20" (50 cm)

Diagram 3b—Module B

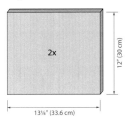

2x

12" (30 cm)

13¼" (33.6 cm)

Diagram 3c—Module B

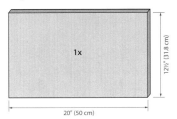

1x

12½" (31.8 cm)

20" (50 cm)

Diagram 4a—Module C

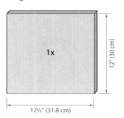

1x

12" (30 cm)

12½" (31.8 cm)

Diagram 4 b—Module C

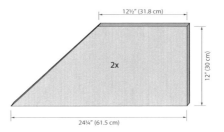

12½" (31.8 cm)

2x

12" (30 cm)

24¼" (61.5 cm)

Diagram 4c—Module C

45° bevel cut

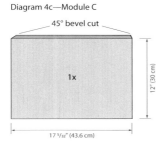

1x

12" (30 cm)

17 ⁵/₃₂" (43.6 cm)

Diagram 4d—Module C

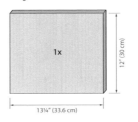

1x

12" (30 cm)

13¼" (33.6 cm)

Diagram 5a—Module D

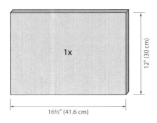

1x

12" (30 cm)

16½" (41.6 cm)

Diagram 5b—Module D

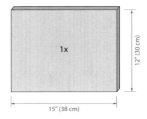

1x

12" (30 cm)

15" (38 cm)

Diagram 5c—Module D

22.5° bevel cut

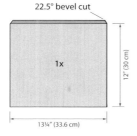

1x

12" (30 cm)

13¼" (33.6 cm)

Diagram 5d—Module D

22.5° bevel cut

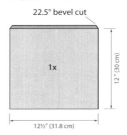

1x

12 " (30 cm)

12½" (31.8 cm)

Diagrams for Modular Structures, pages 22–24

Diagram 5e—Module D

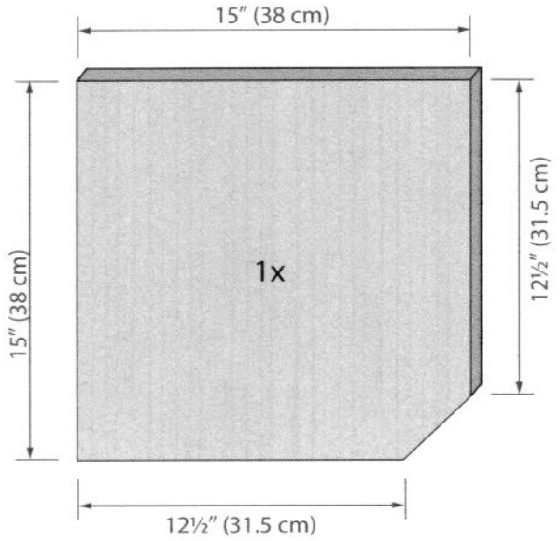

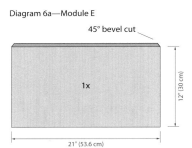

15" (38 cm)

12½" (31.5 cm)

1x

15" (38 cm)

12½" (31.5 cm)

Diagram 5f—Module D

22.5° bevel cut

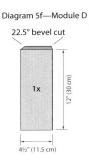

1x

12" (30 cm)

4½" (11.5 cm)

Diagram 6a—Module E

45° bevel cut

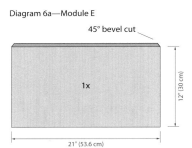

1x

12" (30 cm)

21" (53.6 cm)

Diagram 6b—Module E

45° bevel cut

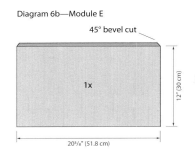

1x

12" (30 cm)

20³⁄₈" (51.8 cm)

Diagram 6c—Module E

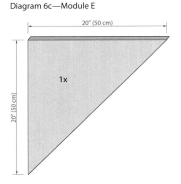

20" (50 cm)

1x

20" (50 cm)

Diagram 7a—Module F

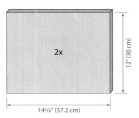

2x

12" (30 cm)

14⅝" (37.2 cm)

Diagram 7b—Module F

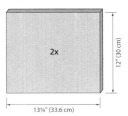

2x

12" (30 cm)

13¼" (33.6 cm)

Diagram 7c – Module F

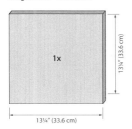

1x

13¼" (33.6 cm)

13¼" (33.6 cm)

Diagram 8—Template for Pavillon Opening

8" (20 cm)

10" (25 cm)

10¼" (26 cm)

Diagrams for the Staircase, pages 35–37

Diagram 9a

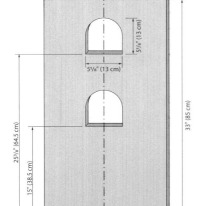

5⅛" (13 cm)

5⅛" (13 cm)

33" (85 cm)

25⅜" (64.5 cm)

15" (38.5 cm)

17⁵⁄₁₆" (44 cm)

Diagram 9b

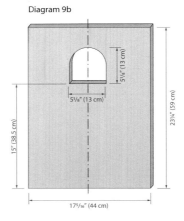

5⅛" (13 cm)

5⅛" (13 cm)

23¼" (59 cm)

15" (38.5 cm)

17⁵⁄₁₆" (44 cm)

Diagrams for the Staircase, pages 35–37

Diagram 9c

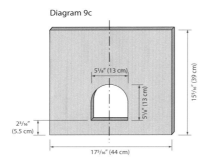

5⅛" (13 cm)

5⅛" (13 cm)

15¹⁵⁄₁₆" (39 cm)

2³⁄₁₆"
(5.5 cm)

17⁵⁄₁₆" (44 cm)

Diagram 10

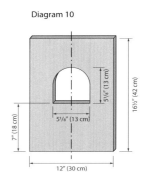

5⅛" (13 cm)

5⅛" (13 cm)

16½" (42 cm)

7" (18 cm)

12" (30 cm)

Diagram 11

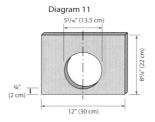

5⁵⁄₁₆" (13.5 cm)

8⅝" (22 cm)

¾"
(2 cm)

12" (30 cm)

Diagram for the Suspension Bridge, page 45

Diagram 12

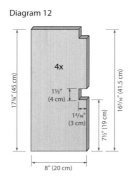

4x

1½"
(4 cm)

1³⁄₁₆"
(3 cm)

17¾" (45 cm)

16⁵⁄₁₆" (41.5 cm)

7½" (19 cm)

8" (20 cm)

Addresses

American Rabbit Breeders Association, Inc.
P.O. Box 5667
Bloomington, IL 61702
(309) 664-7500
ARBAPOST@aol.com

House Rabbit Society
International Headquarters and Rabbit
    Center
148 Broadway
Richmond, CA 94804
(510) 970-7575

Internet Addresses Concerning Rabbit Care, Housing, Health, Poisonous Plants, and More

American Rabbit Breeders Association
(ARBA)
www.arba.net

American Netherland Dwarf Rabbit Club
www.andrc.com

American Society for the Prevention of
Cruelty to Animals (ASPCA)
www.aspca.org

House Rabbit Society (HRS)
www.rabbit.org

Mini Lop Rabbit Club of America
www.miniloprabbit.com

National Mini Rex Rabbit Club
www.nmrrc.com

Veterinary Partners
(information on health care)
www.veterinarypartners.com

Information About Plants in the House and Yard That Are Poisonous to Rabbits

www.thegardenhelper.com/toxichouse.htm
www.hsus.org/pets/pet_care/protect_your_
pet_from_common_household_dangers/
common_poisonous_plants.html

Questions on Living Conditions

Contact your local veterinarian, a chapter of
a rabbit owners' association, or a pet shop
owner. An online search will also provide
information.

Books

Gendon, Karen. 2000. *The Rabbit Handbook*. Hauppauge, NY: Barron's Educational Series.

Harriman, Marinell. 2005. *House Rabbit Handbook: How to Live with an Urban Rabbit,* 4th edition. Alameda, CA: Drollery Press.

McBride, Anne. 1998. *Why Does My Rabbit...?* London: Souvenir Press.

Moore, Lucile C. 2005. *A House Rabbit Primer: Understanding and Caring for Your Companion Rabbit.* Santa Monica, CA: Santa Monica Press.

Pavia, Audrey. 2003. *Rabbits for Dummies.* Hoboken, NJ: Wiley Publishing, Inc.

Viner, Bradley. 1999. *All About Your Rabbit.* Hauppauge, NY: Barron's Educational Series, Inc.

Wegler, Monica. 2008. *My Dwarf Rabbit (My Pet Series).* Hauppauge, NY: Barron's Educational Series, Inc.

3-m. 2008. *Dwarf Rabbits, A Complete Pet Owner's Manual.* Hauppauge, NY: Barron's Educational Series, Inc.

Magazines

Rabbits USA
Mission Viejo, CA
www.animalnetwork.com

Thanks

The author, the photographer, and the publisher thank the company TRIXIE Pet Supplies, 24963 Tarp, for the friendly support for the photo production. They also thank the following people for their help: Mario, Martin, and Christian Schmidt; Stefanie Hartmann; Mona Halboth; Jasmin Berg; Hannes Stieglan; Kim Baeckmann; Scarlett Goebel; Hannes Kuhn; Anastasia Brack; Jenny Almoneit; Viola Welters; Wiesia Krol; Ute Boerner; Pet shop Tierisch In, Eisenach

Important Note

Protection from injury: Homemade structures must contain no safety hazards that could injure the animals.
Nontoxic: Use only nontoxic paints and varnishes for treating wood.
Safety: Pens must be adequate to keep rabbits in and predators out, both indoors and outdoors.

English translation © Copyright 2013 by
Barron's Educational Series, Inc.

© Copyright 2011 by Gräfe und Unzer Verlag GmbH,
Munich, Germany **G|U**

Original title of the book in German is
Spiel- und Wohnideen für Zwergkaninchen.

Translated from the German by
Eric A. Bye, M.A., C. T.

All inquiries should be addressed to:
Barron's Educational Series, Inc.
250 Wireless Boulevard
Hauppauge, New York 11788
www.barronseduc.com

Library of Congress Control Number 2012948410

ISBN: 978-1-4380-0208-8

Printed in China
9 8 7 6 5 4 3 2 1

The Author

Esther Schmidt is an experienced and committed
amateur breeder of rabbits and other small animals.
From the outset, she was determined to provide
living conditions as similar as possible to those of
rabbits in their original habitat. This has allowed
Esther Schmidt to maintain intensive contact and
close intimacy with her animals.

The Photographer

Regina Kuhn is a freelance photo designer, and for
many years she has worked as a photographer in
the field of pet photography. Her animal photos
appear in many well-known publishing houses and
magazines. She also is involved in the production of
calendars and advertising.

All photos in this book are by **Regina Kuhn**, except
for: **Oliver Giel**: cover. All drawings in this book are
by **Claudia Schick**.

Syndication:
www.jalag-syndication.de

1 Dwarf rabbits love variety and adventure. The more opportunities for games, sports, and exercise you can offer them, the less they will be bored.

2 Dwarfs need lots of room for romping, running, and jumping. So provide at least 36 square feet (2 sq m) per animal and regular exercise. Especially if your rabbits live outdoors year-round, they must have a large area for running around and warming up.

10 Success Tips for Happy Rabbits

Our Top 10 tips show you at a glance what's involved in keeping dwarf rabbits. They identify what is needed in order to ensure a long and healthy life for your dwarfs.

3 Before the new inhabitant moves in, the area must be rabbit proofed. Dangers lurk everywhere. All-around protection is the highest priority with outdoor living. Make sure that enemies cannot get in and that the dwarfs cannot run away from home.

4 Hay must always be available. It is the dwarfs' staple food. You also need to provide fresh water and green, succulent foods. Of great importance are twigs and branches for gnawing.